Original title:
The Silence of Winter's Snow

Copyright © 2024 Creative Arts Management OÜ
All rights reserved.

Author: Amelia Montgomery
ISBN HARDBACK: 978-9916-94-606-0
ISBN PAPERBACK: 978-9916-94-607-7

A Canvas of Quietude

Beneath the white, the squirrels bide,
They plot their moves, with nuts as pride.
The world is still, a sleepy show,
While I trip over mounds of snow.

The flakes fall down like feathers light,
Covering paths in pure delight.
I make a snowman with a grin,
He's got a carrot nose and wintry kin.

Portraits of Snowbound Tranquility

The trees wear coats of frosty white,
While birds play tag in frozen flight.
A snowball fight, oh what a sight,
I duck too late—oh what a plight!

The snow plow roars, a beast in tow,
Sweeping the streets with frigid flow.
As children giggle, sleds in tow,
I think I'll join, despite my woe.

The Still Breaths of Frost

In crisp air, my breath transforms,
To clouds that dance through winter storms.
But watch the ice, it's sly and sneaky,
One slip, and I'll look quite goofy!

The world is wrapped, a frosty gift,
And snowmen wobble—what a rift!
I tried to skateboard on this white,
But now I slide—oh what a fright!

Ethereal Dance of Snowflakes

Frosty dancers twirl and sway,
With sparkly moves, they steal the day.
I watch in awe, with cocoa near,
While dreaming of the march of deer.

But outside, hidden under white,
My garden gnomes are losing height.
They're buried deep, with giggles shared,
As winter laughs, I feel unprepared.

Frozen Breath of the Season

Puffs of air like little clouds,
Tickle noses, draw out crowds.
Snowflakes dance, they spin and twirl,
A chilly waltz, a frosty whirl.

Snowmen grin with carrot noses,
Wearing socks, the fashion poses.
Tripping on ice, we laugh and fall,
Winter's prankster, we heed the call.

Serenity in Snowflakes' Touch

Frosty flakes, a snowball fight,
Catching ones that float in flight.
Giggles echo, hearts are light,
Winter's jesters, what a sight!

Slipping down on icy streams,
We craft our wildest winter dreams.
Hot cocoa cups, we toast and cheer,
With sticky marshmallows, oh dear!

The Soft Tongue of Winter

Tongue of snow, it licks the ground,
All in coats, we gather round.
Snow is soft, but sleds go fast,
Breath of winter, whoosh, then splat!

Muffled laughs in leaps and bounds,
Chasing cheeks where laughter sounds.
Winter whispers with a cold tease,
Tickling us with playful breeze.

Silence Embracing the Frost

Stars peek down through snowy nights,
While we bicker over snowball fights.
Oh, look! The cats, they glide and prance,
In this winter wonderland dance!

Gloves and scarves, mismatched with flair,
Winter fashion, we just don't care.
With every slip, a giggle's sent,
As snowflakes cloak the world, we vent!

Serenade of the Cold Wind

Whispers of frost play on my nose,
As chilly breezes hum silly prose.
The garden gnomes, all dressed in white,
Now look like marshmallows in twilight.

Frosty fingers tickle my cheek,
As the wind giggles and begins to squeak.
Pine trees dance like they've got no care,
And snowflakes waltz through the frosty air.

Snowbound Soliloquy

My dog's a snowball rolling fast,
Chasing his tail—oh, what a blast!
I slip and slide, a graceful dance,
At last! A snow angel gives me a chance.

Hot cocoa spills, the cup's gone dry,
With whipped cream mustaches, oh my, oh my!
The snowman's brazen, with a carrot nose,
He's judging my outfit; it certainly shows.

Hushed Footprints in the Snow

Footprints shuffle, a silly parade,
As I follow the trail that the squirrel made.
They lead to places I cannot discern,
Where snacks come from that I never learn.

The snow piles up on my neighbor's dog,
He's a fluffy snow monster, not a log.
With a wagging tail and barks of delight,
He'll throw snowballs back at me, what a sight!

Gathering Clouds of Solitude

Puffing clouds gather, a fluffy fleet,
While I enjoy cocoa by my warm seat.
The cat stares out with a puffed-up purr,
As snowflakes dance, she gives a gentle slur.

Outside, the children tumble and dive,
Bulldozing their friends, oh, how they strive!
Yet in my chair, snug as a bug,
I watch them all, feeling rather smug.

Shrouded in Icy Silence

Whispers dance on frosty air,
As snowflakes tumble without a care.
Squirrels wearing tiny coats,
Giggle while they dodge the goats.

Pigeons puffed like fluffy pies,
Strut around in icy disguise.
Frosty fingers pinch my nose,
Yet laughter blooms where it snows.

Chilled Breath of the Land

Penguins waddling, quite a sight,
In this chill, they feel so light.
Snowmen squabble, hats awry,
In a snowball fight, oh my!

Icicles dangle, sharp and bold,
While frostbitten fingers, brave and cold.
Bunnies leap like they're on air,
In a game of freeze tag, without a care!

Beneath the Crystal Canopy

Under blankets of crystal white,
Puppies prance with all their might.
Snowflakes stick to noses small,
As children giggle and take a fall.

Hot cocoa's bubbling, marshmallows float,
A winter picnic on the snow-coated moat.
Snowballs fly, no one's immune,
To the laughter that brightens the gloom.

Frosty Murmurs in the Night

The moon peeks through the chilly trees,
Nudging the world with icy breeze.
A cat in boots, so proud and grand,
Stalks the snow like it's quicksand.

In the stillness, owls seem to conspire,
With snowflakes falling, their capers inspire.
All the critters are snug and tight,
As the world giggles in the frosty night.

Serenity in Falling Flurries

As flakes dance like they've lost their vows,
They twirl and spin on the chilly toes.
Each one giggles as it takes a dive,
Piling up where the snowmen thrive.

A snowball fight breaks the frosty calm,
Faces painted with laughter's balm.
While squirrels in hats practice their tricks,
Winter's stage is a comic remix.

With noses red like tomatoes bold,
We stomp our feet to keep out the cold.
But secretly wearing socks with holes,
As giggles escape from our frozen souls.

In sparkling white, the world grows bright,
Where snowflakes whisper in sheer delight.
Let's throw caution and snowballs high,
With jokes so bad, they make snowmen cry!

Shadows of Crisp Air

The air is crisp, like a crunchy snack,
A crunch underfoot, oh, what a crack!
While penguins in sweaters strut around,
And giggling snowflakes fall to the ground.

Children dash, like they're full of sugar,
Launching snowballs, each one a booger.
Their laughter echoes, a joyful sound,
While cold-nosed puppies tumble on the ground.

With every breath, we puff like trains,
Our cheeks so red, it causes some pains.
Wearing boots two sizes too large with flair,
We waddle like ducks, but we don't care.

As warm cocoa spills on our mittens and hats,
We decorate mugs with our playful spats.
The outside world, it may be so chill,
But inside our hearts, we're all laughing still!

Emptiness Draped in White

The world dons a coat of ghostly fluff,
But the hot chocolate isn't warm enough!
Snowmen frown with their carrot noses,
As they try to ward off the chilly poses.

With mittens mismatched and boots all askew,
We trudge through drifts, our laughter askew.
Each step a slip, like ballet gone wrong,
With snowflakes juggling, singing our song.

Branches drape heavy with powdered wigs,
While birds wear scarves, and giggle like jigs.
As ice skates glide with ungraceful flair,
The wintery show, a delightful affair.

Yet beneath all this white, the gloom tries to rise,
Underneath layers, we all fake the sighs.
But with every slip, and laugh we share,
Emptiness fills with our joyful affair!

Soft Murmurs of the Cold

In fluffy mounds, we dive and leap,
Making snow angels—you won't hear a peep.
But then the wind sneezes, who knew it could,
A chorus of giggles, misunderstood.

While icicles drip like a frozen joke,
We gather around for the great snow poke.
With cheeks puffed out like bright little clown,
We tumble and trip, but don't wear a frown.

The flakes whisper tales of snowball delight,
As we plot against each other in flight.
The cold may nip, but our hearts are warm,
In laughter's embrace, we weather the storm.

Our frosty breaths weave stories so bold,
In the midst of the chill, we find joy untold.
So let's paint the white with all our cheer,
In this winter land, we have not a fear!

Silent Footprints on Frozen Ground

In the deep white fluff, I trudge along,
My boots make sounds that feel all wrong.
I slip and slide, a sight to see,
Like a clumsy penguin, just not with glee.

Traces of laughter fill the air,
As snowflakes land on my frosty hair.
I dance with the flakes, oh what a sight,
Winter's my partner, though quite uptight.

I hide from the cold with layers galore,
Yet still outside, I tumble and roar.
With frozen fingers, I build a mound,
A snowman smiles without a sound.

But when I turn to make my retreat,
I step on a patch that's not so sweet.
A whoosh and a thud, like a bad joke,
Down I go, with a puff of smoke.

Ghostly Grace of the Season

Frosty whispers float on the breeze,
As I shimmy through with awkward ease.
I challenge the snow with all my might,
Yet trip on my scarf—what a fright!

A ghostly figure in white attire,
I wave at critters, set their hearts on fire.
They scamper away, eyes wide and bright,
Who knew a snowman could give such a fright?

My mittens are bulky, I cannot grip,
Hot cocoa splashes on my winter trip.
With marshmallows bobbing, I can't help but grin,
Though each sip feels like a snowy win.

The winter moon beams down with giggles,
While I dance in snowdrifts, trying to wiggle.
A comedic ballet, or so I'll claim,
In the theater of cold, we're all fair game.

Quietude Wrapped in Snow

Under a blanket of soft, cold sheets,
I step outside, hear joyful beats.
Snowballs fly with a cheeky aim,
But dodging swiftly, I'll win this game.

Snowflakes tumble, pirouetting down,
While I try to twirl, end up on the ground.
Giggles erupt from a distant crowd,
As I act all cool—but I'm not too proud.

A squirrel skitters, it knows the plot,
Steals my snack—now that's not hot!
With cheeks puffed up, I stake my claim,
In a snowball fight, I'll earn my fame.

But as the dusk comes, I make my way,
With frozen toes, it's time to play.
Yet in the stillness of the night,
I laugh at the chaos, it feels so right.

Muffled Cries of the Chill

Oh, winter's chill brings a joyful thrall,
With layers of fluff, I bravely sprawl.
Puffs of breath steam in the air,
As I try to find my missing chair.

The cold has a way of making me giggle,
As I feel the snow and begin to wiggle.
With every tumble, a laugh is gained,\nMy icy antics should be well ingrained.

A snow fort rises, the fortress of cheer,
Though snowballs fly, I show no fear.
I'm armed with snow, with mittens galore,
It's an epic battle—oh, what a score!

As twilight whispers, the fun subsides,
But the stories linger, like snow in tides.
With a grin on my face, I head back inside,
Winter brings laughter—who needs to hide?

Enchantment of the Winter White

Snowflakes fall with a giggle,
They dance like clumsy elves,
Winter wraps the world in white,
As we all trip on ourselves.

The trees wear coats of powder,
Covered like some giant cake,
We sneak tastes, but make a mess,
Who knew frost could be so fake?

Snowmen stand with silly grins,
Their noses made of carrots,
If they could laugh, oh what fun,
They'd tell jokes that leave us scarred!

So we bundle up like marshmallows,
In layers thick, we waddle away,
With cheeks like apples, red and round,
Winter brings its game to play.

Love Letters in Snow

In the courtyard, hearts are drawn,
With twirls and swirls, love's a game,
But each time you try a sweet kiss,
You snowball face-first, oh what shame!

You wrote me letters on the ground,
In cursive, yet it got erased,
A friendly dog thought it was food,
And here I stand, completely faced!

You brought me chocolate, all wrapped tight,
Then we lost it in a snowbank,
Now we search with little hope,
And all that's left is sweet prank rank!

Yet love, it melts with sunshine bright,
We laugh through shivers, it's a sight,
Together in this frozen land,
Our hearts stick like a snowball band.

Reveries in Crystal Form

Nature's jewels fall from the sky,
Each flake a prank in disguise,
They gather on my tongue and freeze,
Who knew frost could taste like lies?

Icicles hang like chandeliers,
Dripping water like little tears,
Each one a blurring, silly sight,
Reflecting giggles, mixed with cheers.

Sliding down the hill with glee,
A bumpy ride is guaranteed,
I faceplant into fluffy piles,
And laugh—because who else but me?

Let's build forts of snow and cheer,
With snowballs flying everywhere,
In this chilly world of laughs,
We create memories to share.

Frostbitten Whispers of Solitude

Winter brings a quiet scene,
But my toes scream like a wild machine,
I wrap them tight, they retaliate,
Whispers of frost, oh what a routine!

Solitude wraps like a favorite coat,
I wander about as if afloat,
The snow drifts dance, but I cannot,
Help but slip, and oh—I wrote!

Yet in solitude, I find my spark,
Creating snow angels in the dark,
With every flurry of chilly air,
I'm just a clown in winter's park.

Time to embrace frosty sighs,
And send a message through snowy skies,
With laughter echoing through the night,
Frostbitten whispers, sweet and spry.

Ghosts of Frosted Moments

Snowflakes dancing in the air,
Chasing each other without a care.
Laughter echoes in crystal glades,
Where snowmen plot their cold charades.

Hot cocoa spills on frosty toes,
A snowball fight? Who really knows!
Tumbles and falls, a slippery mess,
Yet winter's prank brings out our best!

Sleds zoom by, a wild delight,
Racing the wind, oh what a sight!
But watch out for that snowbank tall,
It's a ghostly white and wins each fall!

Winter's whispers laugh and tease,
Footprints tell tales of who took a freeze.
As shadows grow and daylight dims,
We wonder if snowmen really have whims!

The Quiet of Fallen Snow

Fluffy blankets cover the ground,
A muffled world, not a sound.
Cats in coats with mitten ties,
Watch as snowflakes dance from the skies.

Penguins wobble, they slide and flip,
On frozen ponds, they take a dip.
While squirrels wear their frosty hats,
With snowball bombs, they play like brats!

Snowmen wear scarves like fashion kings,
With carrot noses and stick-armed wings.
The chilly breeze brings giggles and cheer,
As frosted moments bring memories near.

Even the trees seem to chuckle,
As snowflakes tickle their bark and buckle.
In this quiet dance, the fun does flow,
As winter plays its chilly show!

Shadows Cast by Frost

Moonlight winks on a snowy plain,
While frosty critters play their game.
Bunnies hop like little fools,
Taking risks near the icy pools.

A snow angel flops, arms out wide,
While snowflakes swirl in a frosty ride.
But watch for splashes, oh what a sight,
As we slip and slide through sheer delight!

With peppermint breath, we laugh and sing,
In this white world, let the joy spring!
While shadows dance with each frosty breeze,
Nature's joke brings us all to our knees!

Is that a squirrel in a snowball fight?
He's hitting a dog — oh what a sight!
With giggles abound, the night's still young,
In winter's chill, we are forever sprung!

Paintings of White Silence

Canvas of white, like marshmallow fluff,
Winter's art is a little bit rough.
Sleds crash into snowbanks with glee,
While snowmen giggle, "Now who's like me?"

Twinkling lights in the glittering night,
Oglers gather, joyous delight.
Penguins waddle in a snow parade,
Creating chaos, a frosty charade!

Footprints lead to mischief and laughs,
Where snowball battles meet with some gaffes.
As voices rise with the icy breeze,
Winter's fun brings us all to our knees!

So raise a toast with hot cocoa high,
To the winters that drift and float on by.
Where laughter paints the silence bright,
In the stillness of frost, we reunite!

Filters of White in the Chilled Air

Fluffy blankets on the ground,
A sudden slip, I lose my crown.
My sparkling nose begins to freeze,
I laugh, oh look, I've got some cheese!

Snowflakes dance like little sprites,
Tickling noses in snowy nights.
I build a snowman, round and stout,
What's this? A carrot's run about!

The trees don coats of crystal clear,
I watch my neighbor spill their beer.
They slip and slide, it's quite a sight,
Oh, winter fun brings pure delight!

Impressions left from boots and paws,
I spy a squirrel, just because.
He does a jig, then dashes away,
In a turban made from yesterday's hay.

Mysterious Calm of Winter's Cloak

A blanket packs the street so tight,
With little feet, I start the fight.
Snowball battles, laughter loud,
I'd even say I'm quite the proud!

The rooftops glisten, oh what a gleam,
A frozen kingdom, like a dream.
But every time I step on out,
I slip and spin, and scream and shout!

The chill is sharp, the air is crisp,
Through frosty winds, I brave the lisp.
Then out of nowhere, here they come,
Two snowmen clash in winter's hum!

With carrot noses, bold and bright,
They dance around in frosty light.
Who knew that snow could hold such cheer,
A wintry show, oh dear, oh dear!

Whispers of Frosted Nights

The night is still, it's way past late,
I munch on cookies made with fate.
The oven's warm, the outside bites,
I laugh at dogs in fur-lined tights!

Footprints tracking a snowy trail,
A penguin waddles, brave and pale.
"Is this my home?" it seems to say,
While I just giggle, sharing the play.

Hot cocoa warms my shivering hands,
As ice sculptures form in frozen lands.
Yet here I trip on my own two feet,
And land in drifts, quite a soft seat!

The stars above begin to twinkle,
While winter's cheer makes laughter sprinkle.
With frosty breath, the tales unfold,
Of snowmen tales yet to be told.

A Veil of Snowflakes

A flurry swirls around my hat,
I look like a walking snow cat!
Each flake a whisper, soft and low,
I chase after all, and see them go.

The sound of crunch with every step,
A ballet dance, I'm quite inept.
But joy's contagious, yes indeed,
In cotton candy fleece, I heed!

My nose is red, my cheeks are too,
I tripped again, would you believe you?
With laughter's echo, the air is bright,
As we snuggle clouds in chills of white.

The world transformed, I lose the frown,
In puffy jackets, winter's crown.
With frosty giggles, we'll stay warm,
Through giggly battles, a new charm!

Tranquility Wrapped in Crystal

Snowflakes dance like fairies bright,
They fall and giggle in the night.
Each flake a joke, a punchline tight,
They land on noses, what a sight!

Trees wear coats of frosted grace,
Squirrels slide in snowy chase.
A winter wonderland, full of space,
With every step, a funny face!

Footprints lead to where they roam,
Each hiding spot feels like home.
But watch your step, don't lose your tone,
Or you might slip and start to moan!

Laughter echoes off the ground,
As snowmen wobble all around.
A frosty freeze turns joy profound,
In this chill, silliness is found!

Soft Murmurs of the Winter Veil

Whispers soft like cotton's glide,
Snowflakes chatter, can't decide.
Should they land, or take a ride?
In this wonder, giggles hide!

Snowmen wear a funny hat,
With carrot noses, looking fat.
They strike a pose, a silly spat,
As birds peek in, where's the mat?

Icicles dangle, dripping slow,
Like frozen teeth in neat row.
A slippery slope is quite the show,
Watch out below, here comes the glow!

Frosted fields, the world a game,
Chasing friends, all look the same.
With snowball fights, oh, what a fame,
In winter's hush, we feel no shame!

A Stillness that Shimmers

Beneath the hush, the laughter grows,
While snowflakes play with frozen toes.
They tickle cheeks, a ticklish prose,
In calmness where the humor flows.

Each flake whispers a tiny joke,
As wind makes trees sway, not invoke.
Branches quiver, the ground so woke,
Nature's call: 'Please don't choke!'

Puffs of snow, we launch and toss,
A gentle fight turned to a loss.
But one more round, we laugh across,
In winter's grasp, we never dross!

Snowshoeing clowns, in mismatched gear,
They tumble, laugh, it's all sincere.
With every fall, we shed a tear,
Winter's fun, we'll persevere!

Ghosts of Frost Underfoot

Through drifts of white, we prance around,
Each step a crunch, a merry sound.
Ghosts of frost in mischief bound,
Underfoot, the chuckles found.

A snowball flies, it finds a hat,
Worn by someone, how about that?
Surprise attack, a squeaky brat,
As laughter rises, just like that!

Winter's air, crisp and tight,
As snowflakes tease and spirits light.
A scene so zany, pure delight,
In every shadow, humor's bite!

When snowmen start to melt away,
They realign, they bend and sway.
Their funny faces seem to say,
'Next winter, we'll be back to play!'

Embraced by Winter's Breath

Frosty hiccups in the air,
Snowflakes dance without a care.
Warm mittens, a hat askew,
Sliding down the hill—Who knew?

Squirrels plotting winter schemes,
Chasing tails, in powder dreams.
Frosty noses and big snowballs,
Laughter echoes as it falls.

Cocoa smiles in every mug,
A secret stash, just for a tug.
Cookies hiding in the snow,
Tasty treasures, cheeky show!

When winter whispers oh so light,
We roll like snowmen, what a sight!
In the frosty jest, we cheer—
Let's embrace the chill, my dear!

A Moment Held in Ice

A penguin slips, oh what a fall,
Ice skates gleam, over all.
Snowballs fly and laughter sings,
Winter's breath makes oddball flings.

Snowmen smile, their carrot nose,
Tip their hats with frozen toes.
Beneath the cover of sparkling white,
Hilarity hides, poised to ignite.

Chilly cheeks and snowflakes caught,
In this wonderland, we've sought.
Wrapped in scarves, we prance about,
Winter chuckles, there's no doubt!

With frosty air and jokes so bold,
Every wintery tale is told.
In moments held where coldness gleams,
We freeze in laughter, chasing dreams!

Chill of the Unspoken

Frosty giggles curl in the breeze,
Snowflakes whisper, "Catch me, please!"
Snow angels flop, wings a bit askew,
Every landing's a laugh, it's true.

Earmuffs hug, keeping secrets tight,
Winter's banter, held in white.
Chill in the air, but hearts are warm,
Sledding shenanigans in every form.

Woolly socks in a cozy dance,
Rascal raccoons in a winter prance.
Snowball fights break the tranquil cold,
Giggles burst forth, never old.

Under the stars, the frosty night,
In the hush, we find delight.
From the chill of whispers, we break free,
In snowy laughter, just you and me!

Serenity Born of Snow

Puffball clouds in skies of gray,
Every snowflake seems to play.
Footprints lead to mischief's door,
Winter's giggles, wanting more.

Hot cocoa spills, it's quite a sight,
Marshmallows clash in frosty light.
Snowflake patterns on the ground,
Nature's humor all around.

A snowman's hat falls to the side,
Twirling as snowflakes glide.
Laughter mingles with the chill,
A winter wanderer's joyful thrill.

Here in this peaceful, snowy realm,
We find ourselves, let laughter helm.
In stillness bright as winter's glow,
Humor frosted, ever so.

Whispers in Frosted Stillness

When flakes fall down like clumsy clowns,
They slip and slide on frozen grounds.
A snowman winks with a carrot nose,
And giggles rise as snowflakes doze.

Cats prance outside, with paws so bold,
Chasing shadows in the winter cold.
Yet they trip and tumble, oh what a sight,
As snowballs bounce, chipmunks take flight!

With sleds that crash and laughter loud,
Frosty adventures draw a giggling crowd.
So let's build castles, tall and wide,
And let the snowball fights collide!

In this stillness, there's joy to seize,
From frosty whispers carried by the breeze.
Amidst the chill, fun comes alive,
In the frosted world, we all thrive!

Veil of Quiet Flurries

Snowflakes dance like a wobbly jig,
As laughter echoes from every big.
The park is a playground, with sleds and cheer,
Where winter's charm brings everyone near.

Cocoa mugs warm with marshmallow fluff,
We sip and giggle, that's plenty enough.
Snowmen wear scarves, one slightly askew,
While kids throw snowballs, giggling anew!

The air is crisp, with twinkling lights,
As penguins slide down the snowy heights.
In every corner, a chuckle can bloom,
While the world outside feels like a cartoon!

Let's twirl and roll in the frosty delight,
Where fun takes center stage, oh what a sight!
In this flurry, we find the glow,
A blanket of joy in the chilly show!

Echoes Beneath the White Blanket

Under layers of snow, whispers play,
As critters frolic in a snowy ballet.
Come see the rabbit, all fluffy and spry,
With snowflakes on whiskers, oh me, oh my!

The world wears a coat, a crusty white gown,
While everyone's bundled up, upside down.
The hot chocolate spills, with a splash and a grin,
As we dive into winter, let the fun begin!

Snow shovels battle with grumbles and glee,
As snowdrifts invite us for a wild spree.
And with frosty cheeks, we all learn to brawl,
In this winter wonder, we'll have a ball!

So take a deep breath, let the cold make you bright,
Funny moments await, in the shimmering light.
With flakes that dance under skies above,
We celebrate winter, a season to love!

Hush of the Frozen Landscape

In a hush so thick, snowflakes conspire,
To blanket the earth in chilly attire.
The trees wear crowns, so fluffy and white,
While critters giggle, feeling frosty delight.

A snowshoe race turns into a stumble,
As laughter erupts, and snowballs tumble.
With sleds zooming down like rockets at play,
On this frozen playground, we all sway!

Frozen rivers turn into laughter tracks,
As skaters slip, and no one looks back.
A duck in a scarf quacks a silly tune,
As icicles hang, like glittering spoons!

So let's cherish each moment, frosty and bright,
With friendships and fun, and chilly delight.
Under the veil of this playful white,
Winter's a wonder that feels just right!

An Embrace of Ice and Time

Cold puffballs in the air,
A sneeze is met with flair.
Frosty whispers in the breeze,
Snowmen chuckle with such ease.

Penguins plotting their grand roam,
Waddles to a snowball home.
Every flake brings laughter bright,
Even the trees dress up for fright.

Sleds fly past with joyful screams,
Chasing after bubbly dreams.
Hot cocoa wit a marshmallow smile,
Winter giggles all the while.

Icicles hang like frozen grins,
As frigid air spins silly sins.
Whirls of snowflakes spark delight,
In this frozen, funny night.

Serene Shadows of Winter

Frosty fingers in the night,
Snowflakes dance in pure delight.
Shadows chase the evening glow,
While squirrels bicker, 'Who's the pro?'

Footprints lead a secret path,
Where snowballs fly – oh, the wrath!
With every toss, a giggled squeal,
Watch your back, it's snowball zeal!

Drifts of white, like fluffy cakes,
Each crunch beneath, a silly quake.
Amidst this quiet, joy abounds,
With hidden puns and playful sounds.

Winter's chill, a jester's game,
Blanketing the world with fame.
Laughter echoes through the night,
As snowflakes cover every sight.

The Calm Before the Thaw

Whispers soft, the world in white,
Pine tree giggles, what a sight!
A snowman waves with frosty hands,
Jokes on skaters, as laughter stands.

Hot chocolate sips and powdered dough,
Fingers frostbite, but spirits glow.
Teasing nature, 'When will you melt?'
Chirping birds are cold, they felt!

Under blankets, snug and warm,
Plotting pranks, a winter charm.
Soon the sun will melt this fun,
While ice cream dreams begin to run.

In the calm, the fun unfolds,
As winter's antics never grow old.
With laughter dancing over the pain,
Goodbye snow, we'll see you again!

Winter's Silent Witness

Crystals twinkling in twilight's glare,
Trees disguised like frosted hair.
Snowflakes tumble, a clumsy blur,
As daydreams swirl in icy stir.

Squirrels gossip in the branches high,
While I attempt my fancied fly.
Clumsy leaps and belly flops,
Laughter's echo never stops!

Winter's chill brings jokes unbound,
As giggles bounce from ground to ground.
Every flake holds a tale to share,
Of funny pranks left in the air.

Silent witness to joy's charming spree,
In frosty pockets, we giggle with glee.
So raise your mugs to joy in white,
With winter's humor, all is bright!

Stillness Beneath Shimmering White

In layers thick, the world wears white,
Snowflakes giggle as they take flight.
Trees wear hats of icy fluff,
Squirrels sneer, 'This is too tough!'

The ground looks soft, a cozy bed,
While penguins waddle, visions ahead.
With each crunch, a shocking sound,
Those sneaky snowmen creep around!

Frosty breath in chilly air,
Do snowballs fly without a care?
Hot cocoa smiles, marshmallows dive,
In silly mugs, we feel alive!

As winter wraps the world in gleam,
We slip and trip, a happy team.
With laughter loud, we share our cheer,
Winter fun? Oh yes, my dear!

Reflections in the Snowy Twilight

In twilight's glow, the world feels snug,
Snowflakes dance like a playful bug.
Crisp air tickles, cheeks turn red,
While snowmen plot their games instead!

Footprints lead to a frosty ride,
Where snowballs fly, and giggles glide.
A snowdog leaps with boundless grace,
Upside down, it finds its place!

Frosty windows hide our grins,
As laughter echoes, and joy begins.
We chase the magic in every flake,
Creating memories, make no mistake!

In this winter wonder, let's not pout,
Let's roll and tumble, that's what it's about.
With every flick of our mittens bright,
Life's a game in the snowy light!

Hibernation of the Heart

When winter whispers with all its might,
Bears snooze deeply, a cozy sight.
The heart hibernates, snug and warm,
In dreams of sunshine, it finds its charm.

Hot cocoa swirls in mugs of cheer,
While snowflakes gather, 'Oh dear, oh dear!'
Chasing rabbits, running late,
In a fluffy jacket, I await!

The fireplace crackles, tales do spin,
As blanket forts become our kin.
Pajamas on, it's time to be loud,
Belly laughs in a fluffy crowd!

So let the cold swirl all around,
In warmth and joy, we're always found.
Winter's hug is goofy and sweet,
With every heartbeat, let's dance on our feet!

Essence of a Winter Dream

Laughter dances on chilly winds,
Snowflakes giggle, oh what a spin!
Sliding down slopes, we twist and shout,
Winter's magic, there's no doubt!

Frosty noses and cheeks so bright,
Chasing snowflakes in the night.
Finding joy in every slide,
Sledding down like a bouncing tide!

Mittens mismatched, hats all askew,
Living the dream, just me and you.
As snow drifts down like a fairy's sigh,
We throw our heads back, watch it fly!

In this season of giggles and glee,
Snowmen grinning, just wait and see.
With a twirl and a laugh, let's embrace the cold,
In this winter tale, our hearts unfold!

An Ode to the Shimmering White

Oh look, the snowflakes dance in glee,
They twirl and swirl, like a wild bee.
Frosty noses, cheeks so bright,
Building snowmen that wobble upright.

Sleds whoosh by, a comical sight,
With tangled scarves, what a crazy flight!
The snowball fights, a playful war,
Laughter echoes, who could ask for more?

Mittens lost, in the fluff they hide,
Jumps on ice, then a slippery slide.
Hot cocoa spills, a frothy joy,
As snowflakes blanket every toy.

So raise a toast, to that chilly show,
Where laughter lives, beneath the snow.
With frozen fingers, we all agree,
Winter's fun is pure jubilee!

Enchanted Stillness of the Cold

The world dressed up in cotton white,
A sparkly quilt, a sparkly sight.
Snow scrunches under happy feet,
As we race through snowdrifts, oh what a treat!

Icicles hang, like glistening teeth,
Watch out, my friend, don't stand beneath!
A snowball flies, a comical whack,
Laughter erupts, then back to the pack.

Fleece-lined hats with ears that flop,
Jumping from snowbanks, a lopsided plop!
Snow angels wave with flappy wings,
Even the winter seems to sing.

Hot soup awaits us, steaming and bright,
Next to the windows, a cozy sight.
So let's embrace the frosty cheer,
And dance in the cold without any fear!

Solitude Wrapped in Ice

In the grip of chill, we play hide and seek,
With snowflakes that tickle and leaves that squeak.
A snowman's nose is a carrot misfit,
He grins with joy, though his eyes don't really fit.

Blizzards swirl, like a funky old broom,
Plowing through yards, a snowy costume.
Pets prance around, in coats that glow,
Chasing their tails, on this frosty show.

Skaters glide with a whimsical flair,
Trying to waltz in the chilly air.
Cocoa spills, look! It's a splattered dream,
But who can frown, with marshmallows that gleam?

Under the stars, the snowflakes giggle,
As kids make wishes while giving a wiggle.
So raise your cups in this snowy delight,
For laughter and fun make the cold feel right!

Echoes of the Snowbound

Frosty flakes falling down,
A snowman frowns with a crown.
Penguins sliding on their bellies,
While squirrels hide nuts in their jellies.

Footprints lead a dance in white,
Reindeer pondering, 'Is this right?'
A snowball fight, a flurry of fun,
Missed your target? Oh, here comes one!

A hot cocoa spill, what a sight,
Marshmallows floating, oh, what delight!
Slippery slopes with giggles and shrieks,
Just when you think winter's for the meek.

So let the snow cover what it can,
With grinning snowflakes and a snowman clan.
Pinch each other, make a joke or two,
Winter's chilly, but laugh we do!

Still Waters of the Cold

Icicles hang like toothy grins,
Winter waits for the playful sins.
A skater wobbles, falls with flair,
Is this ballet or a snowman scare?

Chattering teeth, we bundle tight,
Who knew it could be a snowball fight?
Snowflakes tickle as they drop,
Some folks lose their balance and flop.

The frozen pond's a thrilling stage,
Where penguins strut, earning wage.
Sledding down with leaps and bounds,
Laughter echoes through the sounds.

So, embrace the chill, don't take it slow,
In snowy chaos, let your heart glow.
For even in cold, joy will sprout,
With every little giggle, there's no doubt!

Winter's Gentle Veil

A fluffy blanket covers the ground,
Where snowflakes swirl like giggles abound.
Santa's sleigh takes a tumble so grand,
Elves chuckle as they lend a hand.

The cold winds whisper silly tales,
Of rabbits in coats and sodden pails.
Embrace the freeze with hot cider near,
As snowmen dance, let's all give a cheer!

Gigs of children in scarves and hats,
Mine's too big, that's where the fun's at!
Frosty snowballs, oh what a mess,
But nothing beats winter's funny excess.

So here we are in snow's soft grip,
Zip up that coat, make your next trip.
From snowflakes' giggles to friendly show,
Life's a frosty jest, we all know!

Peace in a Glacial Whisper

Whispers soft in the frosted air,
Chucking snowballs, if you dare.
Under the moon, the snowflakes prance,
While penguins tread in a frozen dance.

Sledding down with quite the speed,
Whoops and laughs, we take the lead.
Snowmen wobble, hats askew,
"Build me taller!" says the frozen crew.

Hiccups from cocoa, a spilling spree,
Mom's gonna shout, "Don't bother me!"
Snowy branches droop with cheer,
Bringing giggles of winter near.

So let's rejoice in this winter spree,
With frosty antics like you and me.
In nippy air, we find our place,
In a hush so funny, let's embrace!

The Quiet After the Storm

Beneath the fluff, the ground does hide,
A squirrel on skis, a daring ride.
Snowballs like cannonballs fly and miss,
As giggles dance in the winter bliss.

Footprints squish, crunch, and squeak,
A frozen world that makes us peek.
Kids build forts, snowmen with flair,
But there's no way to style that wild hair!

The sun pops out, it's bright and bold,
Snow melts like secrets slowly told.
Tricky slips and accidental dives,
A comedy show where nobody thrives!

In this chilly great white maze,
Laughter echoes in soft, snowy haze.
As all things freeze, but spirits glow,
We find our joy in the frosty show.

Breath of the Wintry Woods

In the woods, the trees look posed,
A deer in shades of white doze.
Branches wave with a frosty grin,
And squirrels in parkas gather in.

The air is sharp, it bites and stings,
As laughter hops on snowy wings.
Bunny socks waddle by with grace,
While penguins practice their ice-skating race.

Snowflakes fall like confetti bright,
Landing on noses, such a sight!
The woodland critters play hide and seek,
In a shoveling game, you hear them squeak.

Oh, the chill can tickle indeed,
With winter fun, it plants a seed.
As breath turns to clouds, we find our cheer,
In the woods where winter brings good cheer.

Calming White Hush

A blanket soft, where whispers cease,
A pancake bunny thinks of peace.
Wooly hats bobble in snowy strolls,
While laughter frolics and snow dances, it rolls.

Icicles hang with a delicate grace,
Sending squirrels on a stealthy chase.
"Catch me if you can!" they seem to sing,
While sliding on ice is truly a thing!

Fluffy headgear in colorful array,
Snowmen smile at this clumsy ballet.
As mittens slip off, we tumble and sway,
Winter giggles lead us astray.

In a hush that's not really quiet,
Snowflakes twinkle, it's a riot!
Laughter reigns in winter's embrace,
In frosty fun, we find our place.

In the Grip of Frost

Frosty fingers grip the trees,
Whispers travel on the breeze.
A snowball launches through the air,
Hit or miss, we just don't care!

A snowplow rushes, bumping along,
Its engine sounds like a winter song.
While snowflakes tickle and dance with glee,
Joyful jokes flow like hot cocoa tea.

Frosty noses and cheeks aglow,
Winter tales twist and ebb like snow.
We trip on ice with grace unplanned,
But laughter echoes across the land.

In the grip of a chill embrace,
We trip and stumble, a lively race.
Through the cold, our spirits soar,
It's a winter wonderland, who could want more?

A Blanket of Softness Above

Flakes tumble down like a joke in the air,
A frosty mischief in the chill we all share.
Snowmen wobble, their noses askew,
While sleds go racing, oh what a view!

Children giggle, their cheeks rosy and round,
As snowballs fly, dodging all around.
The cats in the window are having a shock,
Watching the madness from their warm little spot.

Hot cocoa waits, like a toasty embrace,
With marshmallows floating, a sweet fluffy race.
Yet outside, chaos, as people collide,
In snowdrifts so deep, where nobody can hide!

As night falls softly, the moon starts to glow,
It sparkles on rooftops, a magical show.
So here's to the laughter that weather can bring,
In this winter wonder, let's dance and let's sing!

Traces of Time in Glacial Silence

Icicles dangle, like nature's sharp teeth,
With winter's cold breath that feels like a wreath.
Squirrels are hoarding, like it's a sale,
They're plotting a heist for the nuts without fail.

Frost paints the windows, a delicate lace,
While shoes slip and slide in an awkward race.
There's a dance of the robins, all fluffed and bemused,
As they hop through the snow, hilariously fused.

The muffled laughter, it echoes through pine,
Where snow angels make shapes that are silly, divine.
Yet the snowman's hat keeps blocking my view,
As it rolls down the slope and yells, "I'm for you!"

Each flake is a whisper of stories untold,
With winter's odd charm, like a tale that grows old.
As we wipe our noses, and pull on our gear,
Let's cherish these moments, and fill them with cheer!

Echoes of Stillness Across the Fields

A blanket of white covers everything still,
As bunnies hop by, with great fluffy thrill.
The world looks so quiet, yet whispers abound,
With snowflakes that giggle, they flutter around.

Frosty winds dance, and the trees shake their heads,
"Why don't you join us? Let's party instead!"
But clumsy and cold, we slip left and right,
While the snowmen just chuckle, oh what a sight!

Snowflakes are rowdy, like kids in the park,
They tumble and tumble, till it's way past dark.
But hot chocolate beckons with a wink and a grin,
While we ponder if it's too late to begin.

In this wintery realm where laughter abounds,
Each snowdrift and icicle has fun all around.
So hold on to this charm as we dance through the day,
In the echoes of joy, let's frolic and play!

Frosted Dreamscape

The world is a canvas, all frosted and bright,
Where snowmen wear hats that are way too tight.
With noses of carrots that just can't stop bragging,
They boast 'bout their looks, oh, it's quite the tagging!

Snowflakes fall down, as they dodge and they weave,
While the children go flying, oh, but do believe!
There's giggles in abundance, and laughter that flows,
As laughter echoes softly wherever it goes.

Winter's a prankster, with tricks up its sleeve,
It challenges puddles, "You think you can cleave?"
And each time we slip, there's a moment of glee,
As we tumble and roll, oh, how funny we see!

So let's raise our cups to this whimsical day,
With snowflakes as confetti, come join in the play.
For amidst all the wonder, and cold on our toes,
Are memories wrapped up like a gift, with a bow!

Tranquil White Embrace

Snowflakes dance with glee,
As squirrels play hide and seek.
The postman slips, oh what a sight,
In puffy boots, he takes flight!

Chubby cheeks, and noses red,
The snowman bows, a royal head.
He'll tell you jokes, if you press near,
But beware! His laugh's a snowball, dear!

The rooftops wear a frosty grin,
With every flap, the snowflakes spin.
I tripped on ice, thought I could glide,
But hug the ground, oh what a ride!

So grab a sled and take a run,
We'll tumble down, it's so much fun!
In this white world, let laughter soar,
And build a snow fort, who could ask for more?

Hushed Echoes of Ice

Icicles hang like toothy grins,
While winter's chill, it surely wins.
The dog just snorts, then rolls around,
In fluffy drifts, he's finally found!

With mittens stuck, my fingers freeze,
I build a fort, with utmost ease.
But then it collapses, what a blunder!
The snowman laughs—oh, such a thunder!

Neighbors chuckle, having their fun,
Snowball fights until they're done.
A winter's war, with laughter loud,
We're warriors without a crowd.

The trees all giggle, their branches sway,
As snowflakes scatter, in joyful play.
Who knew the cold could melt our hearts,
With every slip, a new laugh starts?

Stillness Beneath the Boughs

Beneath the boughs, the whispers sigh,
As snowdrops peek; they reach for the sky.
A rabbit hops, he thinks it's grand,
Until he slips, does a silly stand!

The world's wrapped tight in cotton fluff,
And all around, it's just plain tough.
Frolicsome cats chase snowflakes bright,
While wise old owls watch their flight.

The crunching sound, it cracks the day,
A tumble here, a snowbank spray.
Frosty noses, and cheeks aglow,
Who knew a chill could steal the show?

Gather 'round the fire, my friends,
We'll swap our tales as laughter blends.
In frosty nights, we find the cheer,
Exploring joys that winter steers!

Frost-Kissed Dreams

In frost-kissed dreams, the night does glow,
With flurries dancing, putting on a show.
The penguins slide, oh what a sight,
Waddling home from a party night!

A cup of cocoa, marshmallows galore,
Cats paw at snow, seeking for more.
But oops! They slip, like they had plans,
Chasing their tails, in frosty bands!

Snow forts built high, with doorways wide,
While buddies shout from the snowy side.
The battle begins, but who's to win?
When everyone ends up with snow on their chin!

So gather up, let laughter ring,
In these frosted realms, where joy takes wing.
Each flake a giggle, each drift a song,
In winter's world, we all belong!

Lullabies of the Snowbound Trees

Snowflakes tickle branchy feet,
Tree trunks sway, a snowy beat.
Squirrels jump, they start to tease,
Dancing round like fluffy bees.

Chubby bunnies hop about,
Wearing hats, there's no doubt.
Making snowmen, six or more,
Each with hats and one with snore!

Icicles forming, a pointy crowd,
Who knew they could be so loud?
They clink together with a shout,
'Take a seat, don't fall about!'

Underneath this snowy show,
Puppies roll in the powdered glow.
Finding snowballs, they then play,
Making friends, hip-hip-hooray!

Winter's Gentle Secret

Whispers ride on chilly air,
Frosty fingers tug, beware!
Hats too big, and scarves that slide,
Waddle like a penguin's pride.

Snowmen smirk with carrot noses,
While chilly wind tickles poses.
Cheeks like cherries, noses red,
Let's not mention the cold bed!

Penguins in a snowy business,
Prancing 'round with snowy finesse.
Their board meetings, all in snow,
Debate on how to glide and go!

A jolly jingle fills the night,
As snowflakes sit and feel polite.
With giggles echoing from the skies,
Winter tricks, a fun surprise!

Muffled Crystals on Bare Branches

In the calm, the crystals chatter,
On the branches, pitter-patter.
They giggle soft, so sweet and hush,
As squirrels come in a sudden rush.

Snowflakes play hopscotch on your nose,
As you walk, they land in rows.
With every step, a squishy sound,
As giggles fly from snow-covered ground.

Pigeons searching for a snack,
Waddle forth, then fool and quack.
With puffy cheeks and beady eyes,
Winter's jesters, oh what a prize!

Beneath the trees, the laughter grows,
Snowball fights in fluffy clothes.
With every tumble, smiles bloom,
Winter's joy, an endless room!

Echoing Calm Over Ice-Kissed Ground

Footsteps soft like whispers tread,
On ice-kissed ground, the world's outspread.
Chasing shadows that pirouette,
With each sound, a giggle met.

Snowmen gather, a silly crowd,
With lopsided grins they feel so proud.
"A snowball war!" one declares in glee,
As giants tumble with joyous spree.

Frosty clowns on the rooftops peep,
As the world falls into a sleepy heap.
A snowflake lands on an old cat's nose,
While all the giggling simply grows.

In the twilight, soft and bright,
Laughter lingers, pure delight.
With snowflakes twirling in frosty art,
Winter's charm—oh, what a part!

Secret Songs of a Cold Breeze

Whispers through the frosty air,
A tickle on your nose, I swear.
The trees, they sway with icy glee,
While squirrels plot their cup of tea.

Snowflakes dance like giggly sprites,
Making snowmen with funny sights.
They wear hats lopsided and wide,
A carrot nose, with nowhere to hide.

The chill brings out the jester's grin,
With every slip, there's giggles within.
The chilly wind just loves to tease,
As kids throw snowballs with perfect ease.

So let the cold breeze sing its song,
In this winter world, we all belong.
With laughter echoing and joy afloat,
We'll make all winter's worries remote.

Enveloping the World in Calm

A blanket white and oh so thick,
Quiet roads become a trick.
We stumble, slip, and flail our arms,
Making snow angels with silly charms.

The trees wear coats of fluffy white,
While cheeky foxes dance in delight.
They leave behind their paw prints bold,
A breadcrumb trail—if only it was gold!

A snowball fight, the battle's on,
With laughter ringing until the dawn.
Each throw a chance at glorious fame,
But oft, it ends in a puddle of shame.

As icicles hang like goofy fangs,
We share the warmth with playful jangs.
In this tranquil scene of outdoor play,
We laugh and cheer, come what may.

Nature's Frozen Serenity

Gentle hush, a wintry scene,
Where snowflakes pirouette, so serene.
Animals dressed in cozy fluff,
Beneath the snow, life's never tough.

A penguin slips on frosty ground,
In its slide, joy can be found.
Laughter erupts from nearby friends,
As winter's whimsy never ends.

A frozen pond, a gliding spree,
Noses red, with joyful glee.
Chasing tails and dodging falls,
In winter's game, who truly stalls?

With mugs of cocoa, warming hands,
We share our stories, make new plans.
In frosty air, we find the light,
And turn the cold into pure delight.

Fading Footfalls on Snow

Crunching boots on layers white,
Every step's a comical sight.
We wobble and slide, an icy dance,
While winter giggles at our chance.

A penguin parade, we strut along,
Waddling to winter's silly song.
Barely standing on frosty ground,
A symphony of bumps, joyfully profound.

Fading prints tell a story bold,
Of laughter shared, tales told.
Sliding down hills, with squeals of fun,
Every run with joy is won.

In this chortling winter land,
We find the silly hand in hand.
With every footfall, laughter flows,
In the wonder of the snow-covered prose.

Stillness in a World of White

In a blanket of white, the world takes a snooze,
Snowflakes dance down, wearing pink fuzzy shoes.
They twirl and they glide, like stars in a race,
But trip on a twig, oh, what a sweet face!

A snowman stands tall, with a carrot for flair,
He shuffles his buttons, pulls off quite a scare.
With eyes made of coal, oh, watch him give chase,
Who knew that a snowman could move with such grace!

Sleds racing by, with a scream and a shout,
One tumbles and spins, oh, what's that about?
Everyone laughs, while they wipe off the snow,
It's a wintery circus, but all in slow-mo!

The sun peeks out, thinking it's time for a change,
But clouds roll in fast, feeling quite deranged.
Snowflakes sit giggling, on branches they cling,
Each one has a story, oh, what joy they bring!

The Breath of Winter's Embrace

In the chill of the morn, the hot cocoa's awake,
Mugs are filled high, with just a small flake.
But watch out for marshmallows, they leap with delight,
They'll bounce off your nose, what a frosty sight!

Penguins out waddling, in a tuxedoed line,
They slip and they slide, oh, isn't it fine?
One takes a wrong turn, in a flurry of flight,
With beaks full of snow, they all giggle with might!

Icicles hanging, like teeth from a grin,
They drip drop a rhythm, like a song from within.
Nature's percussion, all frozen but bold,
Join in the ruckus, feel the warmth in the cold!

As the dark settles in, stars twinkle with glee,
Even the colder days know how funny it can be.
So, dance on the white, embrace frosty fun,
Laughter in winter, let's soak up the sun!

Shadows in the Quiet Drifts

Footsteps crunch softly, in a world made of fluff,
Each step is a giggle, is it really that tough?
A dog leaps ahead, in a frosty ballet,
But gets lost in a snowdrift, oh, what a display!

Little kids tumble, or so it might seem,
Heads first in the snow, like a big snowman dream.
They pop up like daisies, with grins ear to ear,
Covered in white, like it's their grand premiere!

Snowballs are flying, a battle of skills,
Laughs echo loudly, the air's full of thrills.
But watch for the one, who packs them too tight,
He throws it at Santa, in the blink of a sight!

As dusk turns to night, the moon's in on it too,
It slips on its coat, and paints everything blue.
The shadows play tricks, and the snowflakes all cheer,
In this wintery wonder, laughter's our souvenir!

Frost-kissed Whispers of Night

As night settles down, everything's aglow,
The stars have a giggle, with a warm, cheesy show.
The snowflakes take naps, all cozy and sweet,
While snowmen gossip, on their snowy feet!

Trees wear a blanket, of sparkling white lace,
They sway to the rhythm, in this frosty space.
They crack and they pop, with a life of their own,
In this wintery concert, we're never alone!

The chill in the air, pulls laughter from deep,
As snowflakes join in, for a dance without sleep.
A troupe of the night, with a flicker and twirl,
Will pull you to join in, oh, give it a whirl!

So grab your warm cocoa, your mittens and smile,
Embrace the night's whispers, let's frolic awhile.
In a world made of wonder, with joy as our guide,
Who knew winter's chill could be such a ride!

Blanket of Stillness

A fluffy quilt hugs the ground,
The snowmen dance without a sound.
Squirrels in mittens, oh what a sight,
Doing the cha-cha in pure white light.

Children giggle, their cheeks all aglow,
Trying to catch flakes on their nose, oh no!
They tumble and tumble, land with a thud,
Followed by laughter, all covered in mud.

Hot cocoa spills, marshmallows fly,
As snowflakes giggle, falling from the sky.
A penguin slips, does a silly sweep,
While Christmas lights twinkle, not making a peep.

The world outside wears a sparkling gown,
With icicles hanging like a frozen crown.
Nature chuckles, oh, what a tease,
Wrapped in white, it's a winter's breeze.

Twilight's Frosted Canvas

The sky blushes pink as the sun waves goodnight,
While snowflakes pirouette, what a charming sight.
Gnomes look confused beneath drifts of white,
Wondering where they parked their sleigh for the night.

Chimneys puff smoke like they're laughing out loud,
As frostbite tickles and the cold feels proud.
The snow on the rooftops all levels the playing field,
As neighbors debate who's the best with a yield.

Snowballs are flying, but watch out for trees,
They're laughing too hard, they could fall to their knees.
With every big splash in the cold, wet ground,
Comes giggles and joy, oh, what fun abounds!

Twilight whispers secrets, the stars give a wink,
While shadows of snowmen start to drink and think.
The world is a canvas, bright and absurd,
Where laughter and magic melt every word.

Lullaby of the Frozen World

The moon sings softly, while the snowflakes cheer,
As every cold critter cuddles near.
Foxes wear booties, and owls blink slow,
Counting their blessings in the winter glow.

Icicles dangle like glitzy chandeliers,
While rabbits are plotting to make some new peers.
They giggle and hop in their fluffy white bands,
Enlisting the help of their snowball hands.

An orchestra of silence sings winter's tune,
While shadows dance gaily under the moon.
A frosty ballet, practiced with glee,
Where snowflakes applaud, "Isn't this fun to see!"

Thoughts of spring make the critters sigh,
As they dream of warm sunbeams dancing by.
But for now, they delight in the snow's gentle hug,
Wrapped in a blanket, snug as a bug.

Glistening Solitude

Out in the woods, the trees wear their lace,
While deer take selfies, striking a pose with grace.
The world is a shimmer, a pearl on the ground,
Where laughter from critters is joyfully found.

Frogs in top hats sing songs of delight,
While snow bunnies hop, not a single fright.
The laughter echoes in the still, frosty air,
As they play hide and seek, without a single care.

A penguin slides by, looking simply fab,
Waving at snowmen, sad or glad? Who drab!
They all join a circle, a wintery ball,
With cups of hot cocoa, they frolic and sprawl.

As the sun starts to dip, and snowflakes twirl round,
The world glistens softly, a magical sound.
Where moments of joy paint a canvas so fine,
In winter's embrace, they all intertwine.

The Lingering Touch of Frost

Snowflakes tickle my nose,
As if they know my toes froze.
They dance on roofs with glee,
While I sip hot cocoa with a plea.

The air's a giant freezer, indeed,
My breath turns to clouds, what a need!
Snowmen glance with carrot eyes,
Wondering why I'm wearing five ties.

Competing with squirrels for a nut,
As they scurry around in a hut.
I slip on ice, do a little twirl,
Fall in the snow — it's a winter whirl!

The frost leaves tracks where I roam,
But snow at my door, it feels like home.
I laugh with my scarf wrapped tight,
In this winter wonderland, oh what a sight!

Captured in White Stillness

The world is draped in cotton fluff,
Even the trees look too tough.
Each branch wears a fluffy hat,
While the pugs are warming on a mat.

I built a snowman, six feet tall,
Gave him sunglasses, cool but small.
He didn't laugh, just stood there stiff,
Guess he needs a real good gift!

The snowball fight was all in jest,
Until my snowball hit the guest!
Now he's plotting, eyes on the prize,
Is my igloo a good disguise?

We feast on cocoa with marshmallow sails,
And share our most ridiculous tales.
Under the stars, we sip and glow,
In this frozen fun, we've stolen the show!

Whispering Cold of the Night

The owls are hooting all around,
Echoes of laughter without a sound.
As icicles dangled like pearly teeth,
I step out with boots that squeak beneath.

Snowflakes whisper secrets to me,
Of powdered donuts and endless glee.
I jump and twirl, arms open wide,
In this frosty world, there's no place to hide.

The moon is a giant cheesy slice,
Lighting up the snow like buttery rice.
While squirrels debate who's got the pan,
I just stand still, a curious man.

When the night falls, we gather near,
To tell ghost stories, but with cheer.
With laughter echoing into the chill,
In this frosty night, our hearts are still!

Mosaic of a Frozen Dream

The snow created a quilt so bright,
Covering the world, a fleeting sight.
Kids leap in fluff like a furry drum,
While puppies slide and spin — oh, how fun!

Each flake's a tiny, unique work of art,
Some on noses, others fly apart.
I catch one on my tongue, not too sly,
It makes me giggle and sigh oh my!

Grandma's cookies warm from the oven,
With sprinkles and laughter, we're all lovin'.
Snow forts rising to conquer the day,
In the frosty sparkles, we'll gladly play.

As night wraps the earth in a chilly embrace,
We toast to the snowflakes, a snowy race.
With laughter and cheer, we chase our gleam,
In this frozen wonder, we all dream.

Milton Keynes UK
Ingram Content Group UK Ltd.
UKHW030751121124
451094UK00013B/794